I0446488

The
SMOOTHIE
Entrepreneur

Starting and Running a Home-Based Smoothie Business

JEFFREY FERON

TABLE OF CONTENT

1

Introduction

Welcome to the world of Smoothie entrepreneurs! This chapter will dip our toes into the vibrant and delicious universe of home-based smoothie businesses. You'll discover the core elements of what it takes to start and run a thriving venture that not only provides wholesome, nutritious delights but also holds the potential for substantial profitability, all from the comfort of your home.

A smoothie business is more than just blending fruits and vegetables. It's a venture that allows you to concoct and sell a variety of smoothie combinations, catering to the health-conscious, the flavor enthusiasts, and everyone in between.

Whether you're blending up green detox smoothies, tropical fruit blends, or protein-packed power drinks, your smoothie business offers a delightful and healthy alternative to fast food.

The Smoothie Revolution

The health and wellness industry has been booming in recent years. People are becoming increasingly conscious of what they consume, seeking nutrient-rich options that energize, satisfy, and support their well-being. Smoothies have emerged as a popular choice because they provide a convenient way to pack essential nutrients into a single, delectable serving.

Why Smoothie Businesses Can Be Lucrative

Running a smoothie business from home offers several financial advantages:

1. Low Overhead Costs: Your initial investment is comparatively modest, and operational costs can be kept to a minimum.

2. Healthy Margins: Smoothies are affordable to make, allowing you to mark up your prices while maintaining competitive rates.

3. Repeat Customers: If you create delicious and healthy smoothies, you'll attract loyal customers who return regularly.

4. Diverse Customer Base: Your potential customers range from fitness enthusiasts and health-conscious individuals to busy professionals and families seeking a nutritious option.

Why Run Your Smoothie Business from Home?

There are several benefits to starting your smoothie business at home:

1. Comfort and Convenience: You can work in your own kitchen, providing a cozy, familiar environment.

2. Flexibility: Set your own hours, allowing you to balance your business with other responsibilities.

3. Low Startup Costs: Avoid the overhead expenses of renting or buying a separate commercial space.

4. Less Risk: Test your business concept and gradually expand without taking on substantial financial risks.

As we embark on this journey of becoming a successful Smoothie entrepreneur, it's essential to understand the core fundamentals of the smoothie business and why it's a promising venture.

This chapter serves as a foundation for your entrepreneurial aspirations, and in the following chapters, we'll dive deeper into the practical steps required to turn your dream of running a home-based smoothie business into a reality. So, get your blender and let's get started!

2

Setting the Legal Foundation

Starting a home-based smoothie business is an exciting endeavor, but like any business, it comes with specific legal and regulatory obligations that must be addressed. In this chapter, we will explore the essential permits, licenses, and health regulations that you need to consider when launching your food business from the comfort of your home.

Every location has its own set of rules and regulations governing home-based businesses, particularly those involved in food preparation.

It's vital to begin your journey by researching and comprehending the specific requirements applicable to your area. This typically involves interactions with local, county, and state authorities.

Permits and Licenses

1. Business License: Start by acquiring the necessary business license or permit. This is typically issued by your local municipality or county and legitimizes your operation.

2. Food Service Permit: Given the nature of your business, you may need a food service permit. The requirements for this can vary

widely based on your location, so be sure to verify the specific regulations in your area.

3. Home Occupation Permit: Some areas require a home occupation permit, which allows you to run a business from your residential property.

Health and Safety Regulations

Health and safety regulations are paramount in the food industry, even more so when operating from your home. Here's what you need to consider:

1. Food Handling Certification: In many places, you or your staff may need to obtain food handling certification to demonstrate your knowledge of safe food preparation and handling.

2. Kitchen Inspection: Your home kitchen will likely need to pass a health department inspection. This ensures that your workspace meets the necessary hygiene and safety standards.

3. Food Labeling: Properly labeling your smoothies is a must. This includes ingredient lists, nutritional information, and potential allergens.

Insurance Coverage

Consider acquiring liability insurance to safeguard your business from unexpected events. This coverage can protect you in the event of customer illnesses or injuries caused by your products.

Local Zoning Laws

Residential zones often have specific restrictions on operating businesses from home. Ensure that your business activity complies with these zoning regulations to avoid potential legal issues.

Record Keeping

Keep meticulous records of your business transactions, permits, licenses, and inspections. These documents can be extremely valuable in showcasing your dedication to adhering to regulations.

Seeking Legal Counsel

If you're uncertain about any legal requirements or regulations, it's wise to consult with an attorney experienced in food business regulations. They can provide invaluable guidance and ensure that you're following the law.

Navigating the legal and regulatory requirements of a home-based smoothie business is a crucial step in your entrepreneurial journey. By understanding and complying with these rules, you not only protect your business but also ensure the health and safety of your customers.

In These documents can be extremely valuable in showcasing your dedication to adhering to regulations.

3

Setting Up Your Home Kitchen

Your home kitchen will be the central hub of your home-based smoothie business, where you'll craft delicious and nutritious blends for your customers. In this chapter, we'll explore how to design and equip your kitchen for efficient smoothie production, ensuring a seamless and productive workspace.

Kitchen Layout

1. Work Triangle: The work triangle formed by the fridge, blender, and prep area should be free of obstructions, allowing for smooth movement during preparation.

2. Counter Space: Ensure ample counter space for ingredient preparation and assembly.

3. Storage: Efficient storage for utensils, ingredients, and equipment will keep your workspace clutter-free.

Essential Equipment

Invest in the following equipment to streamline your smoothie-making process:

1. High-Quality Blender: A powerful blender is the heart of your operation. Invest in a blender with adequate capacity and durability.

2. Refrigeration: A reliable refrigerator and freezer are essential for storing fresh ingredients and smoothie components.

3. Cutting Tools: Knives, cutting boards, and a good set of measuring cups and spoons are indispensable.

4. Food Processor: This can be useful for chopping and processing ingredients quickly.

5. Storage Containers: Secure, airtight containers for ingredients are vital for freshness and organization.

6. Work Surfaces: Durable countertops and work surfaces are important for cleanliness and efficiency.

Ingredient Organization

1. Layout: Arrange ingredients logically, keeping commonly used items within arm's reach of your prep area.

2. Labeling: Clearly label containers to prevent mix-ups and ensure freshness.

3. Inventory: Maintain a system to track ingredient inventory, ensuring you always have what you need.

Sanitation and Safety

1. Cleaning Supplies: Stock up on cleaning supplies, including disinfectants, soaps, and sanitizing solutions.

2. Hand washing Station: Ensure a nearby sink with soap and paper towels for frequent hand washing.

3. Food Safety Practices: Implement proper food safety practices, including regular hand washing, the use of gloves, and the avoidance of cross-contamination.

Kitchen Safety

1. Fire Safety: Equip your kitchen with fire extinguishers and smoke detectors.

2. First Aid: Have a well-stocked first aid kit on hand.

3. Slip Prevention: Use slip-resistant mats in areas prone to spills.

Energy Efficiency

Consider energy-efficient appliances and lighting to reduce utility costs and your environmental footprint.

Your home kitchen will be the epicenter of your smoothie business, and a well-organized, efficient kitchen will make your entrepreneurial journey smoother. With the right layout, equipment, and a focus on safety and sanitation, you'll be well-prepared to start creating and selling your delightful smoothies.

In the next chapter, we'll delve into sourcing quality ingredients to ensure that your smoothies are not only delicious but also of the highest quality.

4

Sourcing Ingredients

The quality of your smoothies hinges on the ingredients you use. In this chapter, we'll explore how to source high-quality, cost-effective ingredients for your home-based smoothie business, ensuring that each blend is a delicious and nutritious masterpiece.

Local Markets and Grocery Stores

1. Produce Aisles: Local grocery stores offer a wide range of fresh fruits and vegetables that are easily accessible and can be tailored to your menu.

2. Frozen Section: Frozen fruits and vegetables can be more cost-effective and convenient, especially for seasonal ingredients.

3. Dairy and Plant-Based Milk: Look for local dairy products and a variety of plant-based milk options.

Farmers' Markets

1. Fresh and Seasonal: Farmers' markets are a source of fresh, seasonal, and often organic ingredients.

2. Direct Relationships: You can establish relationships with local farmers and negotiate pricing for bulk purchases.

Wholesale Suppliers

1. Online Suppliers: Many online wholesalers offer bulk ordering of fruits, vegetables, and other smoothie ingredients at competitive prices.

2. Local Distributors: Explore local food distributors who can provide fresh ingredients in large quantities.

Quality Considerations

1. Freshness: Choose ingredients at the peak of freshness for optimal flavor and nutrition.

2. Organic Options: Consider organic ingredients, especially for fruits and vegetables known for pesticide residue.

3. Food Safety: Ensure your suppliers adhere to food safety and quality standards.

Seasonal Menu Planning

1. Cost Savings: Seasonal ingredients are often more affordable and have superior flavor.

2. Menu Variation: Plan your menu around what's in season to offer variety throughout the year.

Reducing Food Waste

1. Inventory Management: Keep track of ingredient inventory to reduce waste and optimize purchases.

2. Freezing: Freeze excess ingredients for future use, preventing spoilage.

Ingredient Storage

1. Refrigeration: Proper storage of perishable ingredients in the refrigerator is essential to prevent spoilage.

2. Freezing: Some ingredients can be frozen to extend their shelf life.

Supplier Relationships

1. Communication: Maintain open and honest communication with your suppliers.

2. Negotiation: Explore options for discounts, payment terms, and delivery schedules with your suppliers.

Sourcing high-quality, cost-effective ingredients is a critical aspect of running a successful home-based smoothie business. By exploring various sources, emphasizing quality, and efficiently managing your inventory, you can ensure that your smoothies are not only delicious but also affordable, allowing you to provide the best value to your customers.

In the next chapter, we'll dive into creating a delightful and marketable smoothie menu that will keep your customers coming back for more.

5

Creating a Delicious Menu

Your smoothie menu is the face of your business, and it plays a crucial role in attracting and retaining customers. In this chapter, we'll explore the strategies and considerations for crafting a diverse and delicious menu that appeals to a broad customer base.

Menu Planning

1. Customer Preferences: Research your target market to understand their preferences and dietary restrictions.

2. Variety: Offer a diverse range of smoothie options, including flavors, sizes, and dietary choices.

3. Pricing: Determine competitive yet profitable prices for your smoothies.

Creating Unique Offerings

1. Innovative Blends: Develop a few signature smoothies with unique flavor profiles to set your business apart.

2. Creative Names: Give your signature smoothies fun and memorable names that resonate with your brand.

Dietary Considerations

1. Vegan and Dairy-Free: Offer a variety of plant-based and dairy-free options to accommodate dietary restrictions.

2. Low Sugar and Low Calorie: Create smoothies for health-conscious customers, featuring lower sugar and calorie content.

Seasonal Specials

1. Rotating Menu: Incorporate seasonal ingredients into your menu as limited-time specials.

2. Promotions: Use seasonal offerings as promotional opportunities to attract and retain customers.

Menu Presentation

1. Descriptive Names: Provide clear and enticing names for each smoothie on your menu.

2. Imagery: Include high-quality images of your smoothies in your menu materials and online platforms.

Pricing Strategies

1. Cost Analysis: Consider ingredient costs, overhead, and competition when setting prices.

2. Combo Deals: Offer combo deals or loyalty programs to encourage multiple purchases.

Menu Flexibility

1. Customer Feedback: Be open to customer suggestions and adapt your menu based on popular requests.

2. Limited-Time Offerings: Introduce limited-time menu items to gauge their popularity.

Marketing Your Menu

1. Social Media: Share enticing images and descriptions of your smoothies on social platforms.

2. Menu Board: Create an attractive and informative menu board at your home-based location.

3. Website and Online Ordering: Make your menu accessible online, allowing customers to place orders easily.

Crafting a diverse and appealing smoothie menu is a key element in the success of your home-based business. By considering customer preferences, dietary needs, pricing strategies, and effective marketing, you can create a menu that attracts a broad customer base, keeping them coming back for more of your delicious creations.

 In the next chapter, we'll explore the practical steps to take to ensure efficient smoothie production in your home kitchen.

6

Pricing Your Smoothies

Determining the right pricing strategy for your smoothies is a pivotal decision in your home-based business. In this chapter, we'll explore strategies for setting competitive prices while ensuring a profit that sustains your venture.

Pricing Considerations

1. Cost Analysis: Begin by thoroughly analyzing the cost of ingredients, labor, and overhead expenses. This forms the foundation for your pricing strategy.

2. Competitive Research: Research the prices of similar smoothie offerings in your local market to gauge your competition.

3. Profit Margin: Determine the desired profit margin that will sustain your business and allow for growth.

Menu Item Pricing

1. Base Pricing: Set a base price that covers your cost and provides a reasonable profit margin for each smoothie.

2. Size Options: Offer different sizes with incremental pricing. Larger sizes can command higher prices.

3. Ingredient Costs: Consider pricing adjustments for smoothies with more expensive or exotic ingredients.

Combo Deals and Specials

1. Combo Deals: Create combo options that include a smoothie and a snack or a discounted second smoothie to encourage multiple purchases.

2. Limited-Time Specials: Introduce promotions or seasonal specials to attract customers with competitive pricing.

Loyalty Programs

1. Customer Loyalty: Implement a loyalty program that rewards regular customers with discounts or free items after a certain number of purchases.

2. Subscription Models: Consider offering subscription options where customers pay a monthly fee for a set number of smoothies.

Testing and Adjustment

1. Monitor Sales: Keep track of the performance of your menu items and adjust pricing based on sales trends.

2. Customer Feedback: Listen to customer feedback and consider pricing changes based on their preferences.

Cost Control

1. Supplier Negotiations: Continually negotiate with your ingredient suppliers to secure the best prices.

2. Waste Reduction: Minimize waste by managing inventory effectively and using ingredients before they expire.

3. Efficient Operations: Optimize your kitchen processes to reduce labor costs and increase efficiency.

The Psychology of Pricing

1. Ending Prices: Consider using .99 or .95 endings (e.g., $4.99) to create a perception of lower cost.

2. Bundle Pricing: Bundle similar items for a slight discount to encourage upselling.

Transparency

1. Price Transparency: Be transparent about your pricing and provide clear information about what customers get for their money.

2. Value Communication: Emphasize the value of your products in marketing and customer interactions.

Pricing your smoothies is a delicate balancing act between covering costs, staying competitive, and ensuring a reasonable profit.

By carefully considering your expenses, researching your competition, and adjusting pricing based on customer feedback, you can find a pricing strategy that supports the success of your home-based smoothie business.

7

Marketing and Branding

Marketing and branding are essential aspects of your home-based smoothie business. In this chapter, we'll delve into effective ways to promote your venture, both online and offline, and provide tips on establishing a strong brand identity.

Social Media Marketing

1. Choose Platforms: Select social media platforms that align with your target audience. Popular choices include Instagram, Facebook, and Pinterest.

2. Visual Content: Share high-quality images and videos of your smoothies, preparation process, and happy customers.

3. Engagement: Interact with your followers by responding to comments, running contests, and posting polls or questions.

4. Influencer Collaboration: Partner with local influencers to promote your products to their followers.

Website and Online Ordering

1. User-Friendly Website: Develop a website that's easy to navigate, with a menu, ordering options, and contact information.

2. Online Ordering: Implement an efficient online ordering system that allows customers to place orders for pickup or delivery.

Word of Mouth

1. Exceptional Service: Provide outstanding customer service and high-quality products to encourage word-of-mouth referrals.

2. Referral Program: Create a referral program that rewards customers who bring in new business.

Local Marketing

1. Local Events: Participate in or sponsor local events, fairs, or farmers' markets to increase your visibility.

2. Collaboration: Partner with neighboring businesses to cross-promote one another.

Branding Tips

1. Unique Name and Logo: Create a memorable business name and a distinctive logo to make your brand stand out.

2. Consistent Branding: Maintain a uniform style across all marketing materials, including colors, fonts, and imagery.

3. Storytelling: Develop a brand story that conveys your passion, values, and commitment to quality.

4. Customer Feedback: Utilize customer feedback to refine your brand and service.

Promotions and Loyalty Programs

1. Promotional Events: Run limited-time promotions, discounts, or happy hours to attract customers during slower times.

2. Loyalty Programs: Reward repeat customers with discounts, free items, or loyalty points.

Email Marketing

1. Email List: Collect email addresses from customers to send out newsletters, promotions, and updates.

2. Personalization: Use email marketing to address customers by name and tailor content to their preferences.

Packaging and Presentation

1. Branded Packaging: Use branded cups, lids, and straws to reinforce your business's identity.

2. Presentation: Ensure that every smoothie is prepared and presented beautifully to delight your customers.

Effective marketing and branding can set your home-based smoothie business on the path to success. By leveraging social media, fostering word-of-mouth recommendations, and implementing branding strategies, you can create a strong presence in your community and attract a loyal customer base.

In the next chapter, we'll explore practical steps for handling online and offline sales channels for your smoothie business.

8

Reaching Your Customers

In this chapter, we'll explore various sales channels for your home-based smoothie business, from online delivery options to in-person pop-up stands. Diversifying your sales channels will help you reach a broader audience and adapt to changing customer preferences.

Online Ordering and Delivery

1. Online Platform: Set up an online ordering system on your website or partner with delivery platforms like UberEats, DoorDash, or Grubhub.

2. Mobile App: Develop a mobile app for your business, allowing customers to place orders directly from their smartphones.

3. Delivery Services: Consider offering in-house delivery or partnering with a local delivery service for quick and efficient service.

4. Packaging: Ensure your smoothies are properly sealed to prevent spills during delivery.

Pickup and Takeout

1. Designated Pickup Area: Create a convenient and safe pickup spot for customers at your home-based location.

2. Ordering Ahead: Encourage customers to order ahead, reducing wait times for pickup orders.

3. Promotions: Offer special discounts for customers who choose pickup or takeout.

Pop-Up Stands and Events

1. Pop-Up Locations: Attend local events, farmers' markets, and community gatherings to set up a mobile stand.

2. Event Catering: Offer smoothie catering services for private parties, corporate events, and weddings.

3. Brand Visibility: Use pop-up stands to increase your brand's visibility in the community.

Collaborations and Partnerships

1. Cross-Promotions: Partner with local businesses to cross-promote each other's products and services.

2. Corporate Partnerships: Explore partnerships with nearby fitness centers, yoga studios, and wellness businesses.

Community Engagement

1. Community Involvement: Participate in or sponsor community events to engage with local residents.

2. Feedback Gathering: Use face-to-face interactions to collect valuable customer feedback.

Payment Options

1. Multiple Payment Methods: Accept a variety of payment methods, including cash, credit cards, and mobile wallets.

2. Online Payment: Ensure that your online ordering system is secure and provides a seamless payment experience.

Marketing and Promotion

1. Promote Sales Channels: Use marketing and branding strategies to inform customers of your various sales options.

2. Social Media: Leverage your social media presence to announce updates and new sales channels.

Staff Training

1. Proper Training: Train your staff to handle online and offline orders efficiently, maintaining quality and customer satisfaction.

2. Order Tracking: Implement systems to track orders from the point of sale to delivery or pickup.

Exploring different sales channels for your home-based smoothie business is crucial for adapting to changing customer preferences and reaching a broader audience.

By offering online ordering, delivery, pickup, and pop-up stands, you can provide convenience and flexibility to your customers while expanding your business's reach.

In the next chapter, we'll discuss customer service and retention strategies to keep your customers coming back for more.

9

Customer Service and Retention

Providing exceptional customer service is key to building a loyal customer base for your home-based smoothie business. In this chapter, we'll delve into strategies for delivering outstanding service and retaining customers who keep coming back for more of your delicious smoothies.

Exceptional Customer Service

1. Friendly Staff: Train your staff to be welcoming, polite, and attentive to customers.

2. Prompt Service: Ensure quick order processing and minimal wait times for customers.

3. Personalized Service: Address customers by name and remember their preferences.

Product Knowledge

1. Staff Training: Educate your team about the ingredients, menu items, and nutritional information to answer customer questions.

2. Recommendations: Encourage staff to make personalized smoothie recommendations based on customer preferences.

Communication

1. Clear Policies: Communicate your business policies, including ordering, payment, and refund procedures.

2. Feedback Channels: Provide multiple channels for customers to leave feedback and ask questions.

Problem Resolution

1. Quick Response: Address customer concerns and complaints promptly and professionally.

2. Resolution: Offer solutions that leave the customer satisfied, such as refunds, replacements, or discounts on future orders.

Loyalty Programs

1. Point System: Implement a loyalty program that awards points for each purchase, leading to discounts or free items.

2. Membership Discounts: Offer special discounts to loyal customers who sign up for membership programs.

Customer Feedback

1. Surveys: Use customer surveys to collect feedback on their experiences and preferences.

2. Social Media Monitoring: Monitor social media for customer comments and reviews to respond to and address any issues.

Engagement and Follow-Up

1. Thank-You Notes: Send thank-you messages or notes to show appreciation for customer support.

2. Birthday and Anniversary Offers: Provide special offers for customers on their birthdays or anniversaries of being a customer.

Quality Assurance

1. Consistency: Ensure that the quality of your smoothies remains consistent across all orders.

2. Regular Inspections: Conduct regular kitchen and ingredient inspections to maintain high standards.

Surprises and Delights

1. Free Samples: Offer complimentary samples of new menu items or specials.

2. Random Acts of Kindness: Surprise customers with small gifts or discounts to show appreciation.

Community Involvement

1. Community Events: Participate in or sponsor local events and initiatives to build community relationships.

2. Support Local Causes: Contribute to local charities or causes to showcase your business's community involvement.

Exceptional customer service is at the core of your home-based smoothie business. By going the extra mile to ensure customer satisfaction, implementing loyalty programs, and actively seeking and acting upon customer feedback, you can build a loyal customer base that keeps coming back for your delicious and nutritious smoothies

10

Scaling and Expansion

Once your home-based smoothie business is thriving, you might be ready to explore opportunities for scaling and expanding. In this chapter, we'll discuss various strategies for growing your business, whether through diversifying your offerings, providing catering services, or even opening a physical location.

Diversifying Your Menu

1. Additional Smoothies: Create new and exciting smoothie recipes to attract a broader customer base.

2. Food Options: Introduce complementary items such as snacks, salads, or sandwiches to offer a complete menu.

3. Healthy Treats: Consider adding items like acai bowls, energy bites, or protein bars for variety.

Catering Services

1. Event Catering: Offer catering services for corporate events, weddings, parties, and local gatherings.

2. Mobile Smoothie Bar: Invest in a mobile smoothie bar for on-the-go service at events.

3. Delivery Options: Provide delivery services for catering orders to enhance convenience.

Expanding Your Reach

1. E-commerce Platform: Develop an e-commerce website to sell smoothie-related products, ingredients, and merchandise online.

2. Nationwide Shipping: Explore the possibility of shipping your smoothie products or smoothie kits nationwide.

3. Subscription Boxes: Create smoothie subscription boxes that customers can order on a regular basis.

Extending Your Presence

1. Additional Pop-Up Stands: Set up pop-up stands in new locations or at different times of the day to reach different customer groups.

2. Seasonal Pop-Ups: Consider opening seasonal pop-up locations, such as a beach stand during the summer.

Opening a Physical Location

1. Location Selection: Research and choose a strategic location for your first physical smoothie store.

2. Permit and Licensing: Ensure that you meet all legal and regulatory requirements for a physical establishment.

3. Interior Design: Design an inviting, brand-consistent interior for your store.

4. Staffing: Hire and train a dedicated team for your physical location.

5. Marketing: Promote your new store through local advertising, social media, and opening events.

Franchising

1. Franchise Model: Consider franchising your smoothie business to expand rapidly.

2. Franchise Support: Offer comprehensive support, including training and marketing resources, to franchisees.

3. Brand Consistency: Maintain consistent branding and quality standards across all franchise locations.

Funding and Financing

1. Business Loans: Explore options for business loans, grants, or crowdfunding to fund your expansion efforts.

2. Investors: Attract investors interested in your business's growth potential.

3. Bootstrapping: If possible, use revenue generated from your existing business to finance expansion.

Scaling and expanding your home-based smoothie business can be an exciting and rewarding endeavor. By carefully considering your options and having a well-thought-out plan, you can take your business to new heights, reaching more customers and increasing your brand's impact.

In the next chapter, we'll discuss the financial side of your business, providing guidance on managing finances for long-term success.

11

Managing Finances

Managing the finances of your home-based smoothie business is crucial for its long-term success. In this chapter, we'll provide basic financial advice, including budgeting, tracking expenses, and managing cash flow.

Budgeting

1. Startup Budget: Create a budget that outlines your initial expenses, including permits, equipment, and marketing costs.

2. Operational Budget: Develop a monthly budget to track ongoing expenses such as ingredients, utilities, and staff salaries.

3. Emergency Fund: Set aside funds for unexpected costs and emergencies, ensuring financial stability.

Expense Tracking

1. Detailed Records: Maintain thorough records of every expense, including receipts, invoices, and bank statements.

2. Expense Categories: Categorize expenses, making it easier to identify where your money is being spent.

3. Accounting Software: Consider using accounting software to streamline expense tracking.

Cash Flow Management

1. Cash Flow Statement: Create a cash flow statement that shows the flow of money into and out of your business.

2. Payment Terms: Negotiate favorable payment terms with suppliers to align with your cash flow.

3. Invoice Promptly: Issue invoices promptly to ensure you receive payments on time.

Pricing Review

1. Regular Assessment: Periodically review your pricing to ensure it covers costs, maintains profitability, and stays competitive.

2. Competitor Analysis: Keep an eye on your competitors' prices and adjust yours accordingly.

Taxes and Accounting

1. Tax Filing: Set aside money for taxes and ensure you file tax returns accurately and on time.

2. Accounting Professional: Consider hiring an accountant or bookkeeper to manage your financial records and tax filings.

Cost Reduction

1. Reduce Waste: Implement strategies to minimize ingredient and resource waste.

2. Energy Efficiency: Lower utility costs by using energy-efficient appliances and lighting.

Financial Reports

1. Regular Reports: Generate and review financial reports to monitor your business's performance.

2. KPIs: Identify key performance indicators (KPIs) and use them to assess your business's financial health.

Financial Goals

1. Long-Term Goals: Define long-term financial goals for your business, such as expansion or debt reduction.

2. Short-Term Goals: Establish short-term financial goals, like boosting revenue or increasing cost efficiency.

Continuous Learning

1. Financial Education: Continuously educate yourself on financial management and best practices.

2. Professional Advice: Seek advice from financial experts or a business mentor for guidance.

Managing the finances of your home-based smoothie business is crucial for long-term sustainability and growth. By budgeting, tracking expenses, managing cash flow, and periodically reviewing pricing, you can maintain financial stability and ensure your business's financial health.

12

Smoothie Recipes

To kick start your home-based smoothie business, here's a selection of delicious and popular smoothie recipes. These recipes can serve as inspiration and a foundation for your menu, showcasing the diversity of flavors and ingredients you can offer to your customers.

1. *Classic Strawberry Banana Smoothie*

- 1 cup fresh strawberries

- 1 ripe banana

- 1/2 cup Greek yogurt

- 1/2 cup of milk (or a non-dairy substitute)

- 1 tablespoon honey (optional)

- Ice cubes (optional)

Blend until smooth and serve in a chilled glass.

2. Green Powerhouse Smoothie

- 1 cup kale or spinach leaves

- 1/2 cucumber

- 1 green apple

- 1/2 lemon (juiced)

- 1/2 cup coconut water

- 1 tablespoon chia seeds

Blend until you achieve a vibrant green color and a smooth consistency.

3. Tropical Mango-Pineapple Bliss

- 1 cup fresh mango chunks

- 1/2 cup pineapple chunks

- 1/2 cup coconut milk

- 1/2 cup orange juice

- 1 tablespoon honey (optional)

- Ice cubes (optional)

Blend until creamy and enjoy a taste of the tropics.

4. Berry Blast Antioxidant Smoothie

- 1/2 cup blueberries

- 1/2 cup strawberries

- 1/2 cup raspberries

- 1/2 cup blackberries

- 1 cup plain yogurt

- 1 tablespoon honey (optional)

- Ice cubes (optional)

Blend until you have a rich, purple-hued concoction.

5. Chocolate Peanut Butter Protein Shake

- 1 banana
- 2 tablespoons natural peanut butter
- 2 tablespoons cocoa powder
- 1 cup milk (or dairy-free alternative)
- 1/2 cup Greek yogurt
- 1 tablespoon honey (optional)

Blend until smooth for a decadent protein boost.

6. Chia Seed Strawberry Jam Smoothie

- 1/2 cup strawberry jam
- 1/2 cup almond milk
- 1 tablespoon chia seeds
- 1/2 cup Greek yogurt
- Ice cubes (optional)

Blend for a sweet and satisfying strawberry experience.

7. Peachy Keen Orange Dream

- 1 cup sliced peaches (fresh or frozen)
- 1/2 cup orange juice
- 1/2 cup vanilla yogurt
- 1/2 cup of milk (or a non-dairy substitute)
- Ice cubes (optional)

Blend for a sunny, citrus-flavored delight.

8. Detoxifying Green Tea Smoothie

- 1 green tea bag (brewed and allowed to cool)
- 1 cup fresh spinach leaves
- 1/2 cup pineapple chunks
- 1/2 banana
- 1/2 cup coconut water
- 1 tablespoon honey (optional)

Blend for a refreshing, detoxifying experience.

9. Coffee Lover's Mocha Smoothie

- 1/2 cup cold brewed coffee
- 1/2 banana
- 2 tablespoons cocoa powder

- 1/2 cup of milk (or a non-dairy substitute)

- 1/2 cup Greek yogurt

- 1 tablespoon honey (optional)

- Ice cubes (optional)

Blend for a caffeinated, creamy delight.

10. Spiced Pumpkin Pie Smoothie

- 1/2 cup canned pumpkin puree

- 1/2 banana

- 1/2 cup vanilla yogurt

- 1/2 cup of milk (or a non-dairy substitute)

- 1/2 teaspoon pumpkin pie spice

- 1 tablespoon maple syrup (optional)

Blend for a taste of autumn in a glass.

Feel free to use these recipes as they are, or customize them to suit your unique brand and customer preferences. You can create signature smoothies that showcase your business's identity and set you apart in the world of smoothie entrepreneurship.

13

Troubleshooting and Problem Solving

Running a home-based smoothie business comes with its share of challenges, from supply chain issues to customer complaints. In this chapter, we'll explore common issues you may encounter and provide guidance on how to address them effectively.

1. Supply Chain Challenges

- Issue: Difficulty in sourcing certain ingredients or fluctuations in prices.

- Solution: Diversify your ingredient suppliers, monitor seasonal availability, and negotiate pricing with wholesalers. Consider menu adjustments based on ingredient availability and cost.

2. Equipment Malfunctions

- Issue: Blender or refrigeration equipment breaks down unexpectedly.

- Solution: Develop a maintenance schedule for equipment and have a backup plan in case of breakdowns. Consider investing in reliable and durable equipment to minimize downtime.

3. Customer Complaints

- Issue: Negative feedback or complaints about product quality or service.

- Solution: Address customer complaints promptly and professionally. Apologize, provide solutions, and use feedback to improve your offerings and service. Maintain open communication with customers to build trust.

4. Health and Safety Concerns

- Issue: Health department inspections, food safety concerns, or health incidents.

- Solution: Strictly adhere to health regulations and food safety guidelines. Keep accurate records of food handling, storage, and safety practices. Train your workers on proper food safety procedures.

5. Fluctuating Customer Demand

- Issue: Seasonal fluctuations or unexpected changes in customer demand.

- Solution: Plan for seasonal variations in your menu and marketing. Provide special promotions tailored to the current season to draw in customers during less busy times. Use customer feedback to adapt your offerings.

6. Financial Challenges

- Issue: Financial constraints, including cash flow issues or unexpected expenses.

- Solution: Maintain a solid budget and emergency fund to handle financial challenges. Monitor cash flow regularly and implement cost-cutting measures when necessary. Seek financial advice or business loans when needed.

7. Competition

- Issue: Increased competition in the local market.

- Solution: Differentiate your business by offering unique smoothies, excellent customer service, and effective marketing. Monitor competitors and adapt your strategies as needed to stay competitive.

8. Employee Issues

- Issue: Employee turnover, scheduling conflicts, or performance concerns.

- Solution: Maintain an efficient staff management system, provide clear guidelines, and offer training and opportunities for growth. Address employee concerns promptly to create a harmonious work environment.

9. Marketing and Branding Challenges

- Issue: Difficulty in reaching your target audience or building a recognizable brand.

- Solution: Review your marketing strategies and branding. Invest in social media marketing, community engagement, and partnerships. Be flexible and adapt your marketing to changing trends.

10. Regulatory Changes

- Issue: New regulations affecting your food business.

- Solution: Stay informed about local and national regulations. Be prepared to adapt your business practices to comply with new requirements. Consider joining industry associations for guidance.

Troubleshooting and problem-solving are essential skills for any business owner. When challenges arise, it's important to stay adaptable, communicate effectively, and use each issue as an opportunity for growth and improvement.

By addressing problems proactively and professionally, you can ensure the continued success of your home-based smoothie business.

14

Health and Safety Practices

Maintaining rigorous health and safety practices is not only a legal obligation but a vital aspect of running a successful home-based smoothie business. In this chapter, we'll explore the essential measures to ensure your business complies with health and safety guidelines.

1. Safe Food Handling

- Proper Storage: Store ingredients at appropriate temperatures and away from potential contaminants.

- Hygiene: Train staff on proper hand-washing techniques and ensure they wear gloves and hairnets.

- Cross-Contamination: Prevent cross-contamination by using separate cutting boards, utensils, and storage for different ingredients.

2. Clean and Sanitary Work Environment

- Regular Cleaning: Establish a cleaning schedule for equipment, countertops, and utensils.

- Sanitizing: Use approved sanitizers to clean and disinfect surfaces.

- Pest Control: Implement measures to prevent and manage pests.

3. Equipment Maintenance

- Regular Inspections: Conduct routine checks to ensure blenders, refrigeration units, and other equipment are functioning properly.

- Calibration: Calibrate equipment such as thermometers to maintain accuracy.

4. Supplier Relations

- Quality Control: Regularly inspect ingredients upon delivery to ensure quality and freshness.

- Trustworthy Suppliers: Develop relationships with reliable suppliers that adhere to food safety regulations.

5. Allergen Management

- Allergen Awareness: Educate your staff on allergen sources and cross-contact risks.

- Menu Transparency: Clearly label menu items containing common allergens.

6. Employee Training

- Food Safety Training: Provide employees with food safety training to ensure they understand proper food handling and sanitation procedures.

- Health and Hygiene: Educate staff about the importance of personal hygiene and health reporting.

7. Health Department Compliance

- Permits and Licenses: Obtain all necessary permits and licenses to operate legally.

- Regular Inspections: Cooperate with health department inspections and address any violations promptly.

8. Temperature Control

- Monitoring: Regularly check and record temperatures of refrigerated and frozen items.

- HACCP Plan: Implement a Hazard Analysis and Critical Control Points (HACCP) plan to maintain temperature controls.

9. Emergency Preparedness

- Emergency Kits: Keep an emergency kit with essential supplies, including first aid items.

- Safety Protocols: Establish and communicate safety protocols for staff in case of emergencies.

10. Customer Safety

- Allergen Alerts: Clearly inform customers about potential allergens in your products.

- Nutritional Information: Display nutritional information for menu items.

11. Food Traceability

- Record-Keeping: Maintain accurate records of ingredient sources, lot numbers, and suppliers for traceability in case of product recalls.

12. Waste Disposal

- Proper Handling: Dispose of waste, including food scraps and packaging, in accordance with local regulations.

- Recycling: Implement recycling practices for items like plastic containers and paper products.

13. Employee Health Checks

- Health Reporting: Require staff to report illnesses and symptoms, especially when they could affect food safety.

14. Regular Health Inspections

- Self-Inspections: Conduct regular self-inspections to identify and address potential health and safety issues.

Adhering to health and safety guidelines is a fundamental responsibility for any food-based business. By establishing robust practices, maintaining high standards, and staying informed about regulations, you can ensure the safety of your customers and the long-term success of your home-based smoothie business.

15

Success Stories

To help you draw inspiration and insight from real-life experiences, this chapter features the success stories of home-based smoothie entrepreneurs who have overcome challenges and found remarkable success in the industry.

1. Joy's Tropical Smoothie Haven

- Entrepreneur: Joy Anderson

- Background: Joy started her home-based smoothie business in Hawaii, where she sourced fresh tropical fruits locally. Her love for smoothies and her focus on quality set her apart from the competition.

- Key to Success: Joy's emphasis on using local, fresh ingredients and her dedication to creating unique, island-inspired smoothies attracted a loyal following. She also capitalized on the beauty of Hawaii by selling her smoothies at popular tourist destinations.

2. Max's Mobile Smoothie Van

- Entrepreneur: Max Collins

- Background: Max converted an old van into a mobile smoothie bar and began operating at local events, schools, and parks. He offered a wide variety of smoothies to cater to different tastes.

- Key to Success: Max's flexibility in catering to various events and his use of social media to announce his daily locations helped him build a strong customer base. He focused on keeping his menu fresh with seasonal ingredients and new recipes.

3. Cassie's Smoothie Subscription Service

- Entrepreneur: Cassie Martinez

- Background: Cassie started a subscription service that delivered fresh smoothie ingredients and recipes to customers' doorsteps. She sourced organic ingredients and designed easy-to-follow recipes.

- Key to Success: Cassie's business model appealed to health-conscious customers seeking convenience and variety. By focusing on quality and customer service, she grew her subscriber base quickly, earning loyal, repeat customers.

4. The Green Guru's Wellness Retreat

- Entrepreneur: Sarah Green

- Background: Sarah operated her smoothie business alongside a wellness retreat. She created smoothies with a focus on health and wellness, offering nutrient-dense and detoxifying options.

- Key to Success: Sarah's unique approach attracted customers interested in health and self-improvement. Her integration of smoothies into the wellness retreat experience made her business a destination for those seeking holistic health and rejuvenation.

5. David's Smoothie Catering for Events

- Entrepreneur: David Foster

- Background: David specialized in providing smoothie catering services for corporate events and weddings. He created a diverse menu and offered customization options for his clients.

- Key to Success: David's knack for personalization and his ability to adapt his smoothie offerings to different events made him a sought-after service provider. His reliable and professional approach earned him repeat business and referrals.

Each of these entrepreneurs found success by adopting unique approaches, focusing on quality, and responding to their customers' needs. These stories highlight the creativity and versatility within the home-based smoothie business industry and showcase how you can tailor your own path to success.

CONCLUSION

In the deliciously fulfilling conclusion of "The Smoothie Entrepreneur: Starting and Running a Home-Based Smoothie Business," you've sipped through a whirlwind of entrepreneurial wisdom and fruity inspiration. As you stir the final pages of this book, I hope you're equipped not just with the knowledge but also the passion to blend your dreams into a thriving smoothie business.

Remember, creating a successful home-based smoothie business isn't just about concocting delicious blends; it's about stirring innovation, nurturing customer connections, and pouring your heart into every glass.

As you embark on this flavorful journey, relish the flexibility and creativity that come with entrepreneurship. Your kitchen isn't just a workspace; it's the hub of innovation where you mix, match, and craft smoothie masterpieces. Embrace this space and let your imagination flow like the fruits in your blender.

In the world of entrepreneurship, every challenge is an opportunity to add a new ingredient to your recipe for success. Adaptability and resilience are your secret ingredients. From sourcing the freshest ingredients to creating irresistible flavors, your journey will be as diverse as the fruits in your smoothies.

Remember, your smoothie business is not just about selling a drink; it's about serving a healthier lifestyle, fostering community, and spreading joy, one sip at a time. Each interaction with a customer is a chance to brighten their day and leave a lasting impression.

As you dive into the world of home-based smoothie entrepreneurship, keep your enthusiasm blended with a pinch of patience. Rome wasn't built in a day, and neither is a successful business. Celebrate the small victories, learn from the challenges, and let each experience enrich your entrepreneurial journey.

In closing, may your smoothies tantalize taste buds, your entrepreneurial spirit remain as fresh as your ingredients, and your business blend into a refreshing success story. Cheers to crafting not just smoothies but a legacy that leaves a lasting, flavorful impact on the world.

Here's to your entrepreneurial adventure, where every sip is a step closer to realizing your dreams, and every blend is a testament to your passion for making the world a healthier, tastier place!

JEFFREY FERON

Author

Meknatureconcept@gmail.com.

Thank you for choosing this book, if you feel this book is valuable, kindly consider leaving us a review on Amazon. Your feedback is critical to me and others looking for help related to the same book.

www.ingramcontent.com/pod-product-compliance
Lightning Source LLC
Chambersburg PA
CBHW062247290526
45794CB00006B/2444